T0147376

# Rescued
# And
# Redirected

*Great words of encouragement inspired by the Holy Spirit!!*

By

Evangelist Jessie Clay

## iUniverse, Inc.
New York   Bloomington

**Rescued And Redirected**
**Cast Down But Not Destroyed!!**
*Words of encouragement inspired by the Holy Spirit!*

*iUniverse books may be ordered through booksellers or by contacting:*

*iUniverse*
*1663 Liberty Drive*
*Bloomington, IN 47403*
*www.iuniverse.com*
*1-800-Authors (1-800-288-4677)*

*Edited by Mrs. Suzanna Thompson*

*ISBN: 978-1-4401-1138-9 (sc)*
*ISBN: 978-1-4401-1139-6 (e)*

*Printed in the United States of America*

*iUniverse rev. date:1/27/2009*

# Contents

# Step into MY Poetry

# *Acknowledgements*

Thanks to Almighty God who has given me the vision for this project. Encouraging others is the focus of my ministry. Like Paul I am persuaded that I am an encourager. Because I was once blind but I can truly say, now I see.

I would also like to praise God for my husband Joe Clay who always helps in whatever way that he can to make my dreams a reality, my children Tracy & (Jay) Wilson, James & (Antanetta) Binns and their families, my pastor Chester and Lady Betty Witherspoon and all of my family members, church family, friends and anyone who has been a support to this ministry.

One day during the time that I was spiritually blind like blind Bartimaeus I began to shout out to Jesus asking Him to have mercy on me and the Lord heard my cry and rescued me. I picked up the Bible and begin to read the Word of God. I read until I found a scripture that said: "Therefore take no thought, saying what we shall eat? Or what shall we drink? Or wherewithal shall we be cloth?"

Matthew 6:32 says, "For your heavenly father knows that ye have need of all these things." I couldn't stop reading…I ran into Psalms the 23rd chapter where David gives his testimony of what the Lord had done for him. I read Psalms 51:10, and through prayer and the Word of God, I gained my spiritual sight.

# Introduction

My name is Evangelist Jessie Clay, a native of Arkansas. I was born in the country and raised on the farm, a wife, a mother, a grandmother, a Christian Educator, a Gospel Recording Artist currently serving as a Church School Teacher and a member of the Ministerial Staff at the New Home Baptist Church 300 South Street, Crawfordsville, AR under the leadership of Pastor Chester Witherspoon.

Like everyone else, I have had my share of life crisis. But I can truly say that because of Christ I can say the same thing that Paul said. I have never seen the righteous forsaken nor his seed begging bread. It was truly a blessing to be kept by God's love.

There has never been a time in my life where the Lord stopped blessing me. He brought me through my entire tests and trials and I can say that he has never failed me yet. When I think of the goodness of Jesus and all that He has done for me my soul cries out hallelujah.

God has blessed me to know that not everyone has my best interest at hand but nevertheless: He never comes short of his mercy and grace toward me. I am glad that He didn't give up on me. He made me to lie down in green pastures.

# Rescued And Redirected!

"Behold, the Lord's hand is not shortened, that it cannot save: neither his ear heavy that it cannot hear." After being raised in a faith based home, like many of you, once I became an adult and life didn't go as I felt it should, after all the hurt, pain, and disappointments, I started trying to help God out with what I thought was best for my life.

I started practicing living out of the will of God, not knowing like I know now that whatever I needed was already in the will of God. Living in sin caused me not to be able to sleep well at night. I would have dreams that I was sleeping in a bed of snakes and I spent the entire night trying to keep from being bitten by one of them.

I know that if you are reading this book you know that the Lord was chastening me. He succeeded because he got my attention after so many nights of this. One thing that he would do in every dream: He would allow me to escape being bitten by the snakes. I knew that this was a signal from God that I would get the victory over the enemy if I would take heed to His warnings.

I was just out on life's ocean in my own little ship, but how many of you know that sometimes the ship wrecks. I will forever believe that God allowed my ship to wreck so that He could personally rescue and redirect me. I do testify today that I was sinking deep in sin like many of you are now or were.

I always stayed in church hoping that someday something would be said and I would be freed from the lust of the flesh, the lust of the eyes, and the pride of life.

The Lord looked beyond all of my faults and saw my needs and gave me more than double for my trouble. Everything that the devil had stolen from me, God gave it all back to me. I got my joy back, my peace, and the strength to pull; now I am free.

I am writing about this because I know that there are so many others who are putting themselves in wrong positions trying to make ends meet; you have gotten so lonely, been so mistreated, so disappointed and just made a mess out of your life.

I want to encourage you to stop trying to figure out what God has already worked out on your behalf. You are just as important as anyone else and God loves you. When life's problems seem to overtake you turn to God who holds the answer to all of your problems.

The more I share my testimony with others the freer I get in my spirit because I am no longer bound by what the enemy thinks or say about me. There are many women and men going through the same type of situation or worse but they are bound by their situation and have too much pride or maybe fear to share with others.

As a mature Christian I looked at Paul who was ship wrecked as he went about doing his own thing. When he started out his name was Saul, he was trained in the laws and traditions of the Jewish faith.

Paul first appears at the stoning to death of Stephen, after that he got himself into persecuting the Church. This lets me know that we are affected by the bad things that happen in our lives that we don't understand and that we don't know how to deal with.

Paul started entering into men's and women's homes dragging them off to prison just because they confessed to be a Christian. He went to the high priest, and got a letter to the brothers in Damascus, authorizing him to; bind believers and bring them back to Jerusalem to be thrown in jail. As he journeyed, he came near Damascus and God allowed his ship to wreck right then and there.

The Bible says in Acts 9 that suddenly around noonday a light from heaven shined round about him. This light was so intense until it blinded him: and he fell to the earth, and heard a voice saying unto him, Saul, Saul why persecute thou me?

And he said, "Who art thou, Lord? And the Lord said I am Jesus whom thou persecute. And he trembled and was astonished, and asked Lord what will thou have me to do? At that point Paul was rescued and redirected. He was told to go to Damascus where he was headed and there he would be told what to do.

When God rescues and redirects us like Paul and myself, we must be obedient to what God orders us to do if we want to receive what God has in store for us. You will see in this story, when Paul had done all that he was required to do, his whole life changed and he regained his sight and became a witness for Christ.

I was redeemed that very day when my spiritual eyes came open and I could tell everyone that I met what the spirit had said to me. It said that I once was blind but now I see. I called my girlfriend, of 36 years, Betty Witherspoon and I said to her, "Betty, I once was blind but now I see."

She had been there for me so many times before. She would always encourage me and as always, she didn't put me down but once again she helped me up. Before that I had eyes but I could only see the things that were not of Christ.

I began to seek the Lord, all the more, because I knew he had a blessing with my name on it, and I was right. When I surrendered my life to Him, I no longer had to try to find a way to get bills paid, going through so many changes, being treated any kind of way, and yet the bills still needed to be paid. People tend to look down on you when you are down and then they can't stand it when the Lord begins to raise you up.

I must tell you that when the Lord changed my life I was forced to let go of everybody that didn't want to follow the spiritual vision that I had received. The enemy was very angry with me. Some that I used to live in sin with no longer wanted to have anything to do with me because I made Jesus my choice.

It was all good though because the Lord gave me some new friends, some new sisters and brothers, a husband, a house that I did not build as He promised in the Word that He would do if I lived for him and when I lay down at night He gives me sweet sleep.

"Happy is the man whom God corrects: therefore despise not thou the chastening of the almighty: For He makes sore, and binds up: he wounds and his hands make whole." (Job 5:17-18) I am so glad that God used his rod of correction on me, on this side of the grave.

We all need correcting sometimes and we as Christians would be better off if we would recognize that and not be so busy pointing out others faults. When God corrects us He is preparing us for a kingdom life.

# Let It Go!!!

Are you carrying a grudge? I've noticed in my ministry that there are so many broken relationships and most times we all play the blame game because no one wants to be accountable for their own actions. We have family members against family members and we justify why we should cut all ties with them, and then we solicit other family members to join in with us pitting one family member against the other.

I encourage you if you see yourself in this passage, just let it go or maybe just deal with it. Don't let your dark past rob you of the bright feature that God has destined just for you. See you must be aware that Satan made a public announcement that he is going to and fro up and down the earth to see who he can devour.

The word "devours" means to destroy. He is looking to destroy relationships, minds, marriages, churches etc. We must be on guard at all times. Because no one is exempt from Satan's attacks. I don't care how much money you have, how long you've been married, how long you've been in church or on your job.

Satan will stop at nothing trying to destroy you, for he said it himself that his plan is to destroy you. Since you know what Satan's plans are for your life, have you put together a plan to conquer him?

Forgiveness is what Jesus Christ requires of us. We are so quick to run out of the number of times that we want to forgive others before we decide that's it, I can't forgive them anymore. I am so glad that Jesus has more compassion toward us than that.

The word of God said that if we don't forgive others for their offenses, He will not forgive us. Matthews 6:14-15 "For if ye forgive men their trespasses, your heavenly Father will also forgive you: But if ye forgive not men their trespasses, neither will your Father forgive you."

Remember, you don't ever haft to worry about how someone is treating you because you will not be held accountable for that. But don't ever forget that what you do to others, you will be held accountable for on that day when you shall stand before Jesus the great judge. For every careless word that you have spoken you will be held accountable.

"The good man brings good out of the good stored up in him, and the evil man brings evil out of the evil stored up in him. But I tell you men will have to give account." (Matthew 12:35-36) In these scriptures, Jesus reminds us that the things we say reveals what's in our hearts.

What kind of words come from your mouth? Only you need to answer this question but I can tell you that whatever comes out of your mouth is a reflection of what your heart is really like.

You need to get your speech cleansed by allowing the Holy Spirit to fill you with God's love and a new attitude. Sometimes we are so mean because there is a struggle within us, no one really wants to be around us because we haven't dealt with our past hurts and because we hurt we want to make sure others are hurting too.

The Word of God cautions us in I Thessalonians 5:15 not to pay back evil for evil; instead we need to try to be helpful to the one that hurts us. The simplest way to say this is, don't try to get even with anyone who has caused you hurt just let go and let God.

# Healing Your Heart

There are times in our lives that we have heart trouble, and it has nothing to do with the heart valves or congestive heart failure; however, it does have a great effect on the way our blood flows. Some say it causes their blood to boil; I just need to tell you that you need to do all that you can to heal your heart. Most times it all stems from something that happened to us in the past.

If your symptoms are depression, hypertension, diabetes, and/or body aches, it could be that you have not been watching your intake of painful situations. Carrying excess baggage will give you heart problems and make you really tired and sluggish.

What's in your baggage? Could it be un-forgiveness, jealousy, envy, strife, or the weight of a previous marriage? Are there step-children or step-parents involved, ex-husband or wife, or do you have baby momma drama? If you suffer from any of these symptoms, you should consider getting healing for your heart.

"For where envy and strife is, there is confusion and every evil work." (James 3:16) If you really look at this you can see how Satan uses both envy and strife as his weapon to destroy relationships. When these two tools are used we become obsessed and have a serious desire to find ways to afflict pain upon the person that we are holding anger in our heart for.

We lay awake at night pondering and breathing out bitterness because we feel like we really need to accomplish what the enemy has planted in our hearts to do to the one that we have found fault in according to our own judgment.

The heart that needs healing is not the heart within your chest, because that's only a pump designed to direct the flow of your blood through your body. You need to be transformed by the renewing of your mind, and then your heart will be healed.

"Keep thy heart with all diligence; for out of it are the issues of life." Proverb 4:23. We need to make sure we concentrate on the things that will keep us on the right path. Keep your eyes on your goal, and make sure that you are not side tracked by everything that you see along the way.

The heart is where our affections and emotions are; therefore, we must be very careful not to let our feelings of love dictate to us how we should live. If we are not careful, our affection will influence everything else in our lives.

Remember that the eyes of the Lord are in every place, beholding the evil and the good. He knows our thoughts afar off. The Lord is watching everywhere; He knows every move that we make; and He knows every evil thought that crosses our mind.

Free yourself from all of your past bondage so that you will not be hindered any longer, because once the enemy knows that he can no longer get a reaction when he reminds you of your past, he will have to flee for a season. I can say this because there was a time where I felt that I was bound by almost everything.

I was bound by what others thought about me, if they were going to accept me, what they were going to say about me and even how they felt about me. My heart really needed to be healed at that time.

I would go out of my way to do things for others just so I could be accepted. Finally, I noticed no matter what I did, nothing was good enough. 1st Peter 5:7 says that I could cast all of my cares upon Him; for he cares for me. That's when I let Him have all of my worries, concerns and cares; in other words I took everything to God in prayer and He healed my heart.

# *Discerning the Seasons!*

To everything there is a season, a time for every purpose under the sun, a time to be born, a time to die, a time to plant, a time to pluck up what was planted, a time to weep, a time to laugh, a time to keep silence, and a time to speak.

The word "time" simply means a period or space. If we do not know the time or the seasons, we do not know the purpose of God for our lives. Therefore, we cannot be co…laborers with Christ, and are now in danger of working the works of the flesh.

Thank God that nothing stays the same. Everything changes. Sometimes during the seasons it's difficult and sometimes painful, but we can be sure that whatever comes with a season also ends with that season. Just think about a tornado season lasting for the entire four seasons, and then you will begin to appreciate change.

Hopefully, you are not doing the same thing today that you were doing ten years ago, five years ago, or even one year ago. Each season brings something different. It can bring worry, but on the other hand it can bring hope. It can bring happiness, and then again, it can bring sadness. What I am saying is, we live in a world of un-ending changes.

The evidence of change is everywhere. "If any man be in Christ, he is a new creature: old things are passed away; behold all things are become new." (2nd Corinthians 5:17) Seasons have never stayed the same. Since creation, they've always changed, because the Word of God says that there is winter, spring, summer, and fall.

Have you ever noticed how when one season closes, we are moved right into the next? We have no control over that transformation. In our lives, we must notice the signs that signals us when a season is about to close. This will prevent us from getting stuck in a season.

We must accept the seasons that God has put in place for us, because change can be quite good. Please understand that God has made everything beautiful in its own time. Even the painful things in our lives are set in place by God; everything has its purpose.

Remember this, God knows the plans that He has for our lives, and he always puts us where he wants us to be in his plan. I want to drop this in your spirit. If you are still going to the same ungodly places that you have always gone to, and you are doing the same old ungodly things that you've always done, you are not a discerner of the seasons.

I want to tell you, though, that it's never too late…I say that because Jesus still forgives and saves. If you look around and you have on the same mini skirt that your teenage daughter has on, you're in the wrong season. If you are a said to be woman of God, and you are still wearing clothing that puts more breasts and thighs on display than we can see at the neighborhood grocery store, your clothing fitting so tight that your body appears to be sitting down even when you are walking, you are stuck in a season. Because when Jesus has touched your life, nothing remains the same. According to the scripture everything changes.

I made the change and the things that I used to do, I don't do anymore and I don't even desire to do them. The places that I used to go, thank God I don't go there anymore. We should not appear to be women of the world, if we are no longer a part of the world. You must be aware that your outer appearance gives off signal as to what you are like on the inside.

# A Woman of God Is More Precious Than Rubies!

Proverbs 31 refers to "her" as a virtuous woman whose price is far above rubies. A virtuous woman is a woman that is righteous, excellent in morals, courage, and effective in power. She plans ahead and she is worthy to be praised. This woman has so much going for herself; she is truly a role model for all women everywhere.

We see that she wasn't just a house wife, she was a hard worker. She respected her husband. A woman that cared for others, had foresight, of success, great compassion, strong character, great wisdom, many skills and honors...this woman is really worthy to be praised.

She demonstrated self-worth by the way she dressed, because she didn't dress for people to notice her. She dressed modestly...she doesn't flirt; neither does she use seductive postures to get others to admire her. This woman was confident of herself. She knew that the joy of the Lord was her strength, and she realized that everything that she had belonged to God.

She knew that she could do nothing of herself, but with God all things were possible. Her husband trusted her and her way of thinking, and she received praise from those that knew her best, her husband and her children. She does not eat bread of idleness. In other words, she is not limited by anyone. Evaluate yourself based upon the character of this woman, and you might want to keep the score to yourself. Women of God, we don't have to go out to church or any other place dressed so seductive in order to gain a husband.

With not only our cleavage showing, but our entire breast, outfits so tight that every crack, role, curve and corner can be seen. Because we see, in the story of the virtuous women, how valuable we are, if we practice to be what God would have us to be. God made us because man needed us as a companion therefore; we are valuable.

Does your character reflect that of a virtuous woman? When we become women of God, He has our best interest at heart. Anything that you need, you can ask believing that you receive them and it's yours. We don't have to settle for less. What I mean by that is if you need a husband ask God; He will give him to you. I am a witness to that.

Mark 11:24 says, "Therefore I say unto you, whatsoever things you desire when you pray, believe that you receive them, and you shall have them." Women of God, it is time for us to regain our focus and raise the standard for ourselves. One thing that I've learned and want to pass on is we do not have to expose ourselves the way we do in order to get the man that God has made for us.

You don't even have to sleep in a negligee night gown, because it's really not your body that keeps this man interested in you. I encourage you to keep your inside right with God, and the rest is history. Please don't get me wrong because I didn't say don't sleep in a negligee.

I just needed to remind you that you are beautiful on the inside if you are a woman of God. Go ahead though "Sista" and do what you need to do in order to put that extra spice into your marriage.

# *Guard Your Tongue!!*

James compares the damage that the tongue can do to a raging fire…the tongue's wickedness has its source in hell itself. The Bible gives sound doctrine about the tongue and the power that it has; it even says that "life and death is in the power of the tongue." (Proverb 18:21)

Therefore, we need to be careful of how we gossip and spread rumors about others, because these things are both harmful and damaging. We must be aware of all the people that will be hurt by what we have said co…workers, family members or anyone that's around you-even you.

You see, a few words spoken in a few minutes can destroy relationships that it took years to build. James 1:26 says, "If any man considers himself religious and yet does not keep a tight rein on his tongue, he deceives himself and his religion is worthless."

Proverb 13:3 says, "He who guards his lips, guards his life, but he who speaks rashly will come to ruin." I have learned that once you speak, you cannot take back what you have said. This tells me how important it is for us to guard our tongues. In other words, we must keep our mouths closed and stay out of trouble.

We must be responsible for our own tongue, because it is so not Christ…like to allow our tongue to run rampant. If we don't guard our tongue, we could be guilty of blessing and cursing with the same tongue.

James 3:9-10 says these things ought not to be so. Be careful not to be drawn into conversation during lunch breaks, church picnics, women's conferences, family reunions, etc. When we are trying to win favor with some, we put others down to make ourselves look good.

This reflects a sense of insecurity and a loss of self-worth, along with low self-esteem. God has people who will love you just the way you are. We need to cease from trying to be accepted by those who reject us, and accept what God allows.

God will always place someone in your life that is genuine in His love, has the same type of spirit you have, along with the same common goal that you have. In other words, we should hang with our kind. Stop trying to get in where we don't fit in.

"Let your conversation always be full of grace, seasoned with salt, so that you may know how to answer everyone." Colossians 4:6 we should fill our minds with good words. Before we start spreading something that someone else has said, we do need to find out if it's true.

I encourage you to reframe from using that old thing about it came from a reliable source, because no matter how well we think that we know a person sometime they pass on what someone else has said unaware of it not being true.

Satan uses the tongue to divide us and to pit us against one another. We should only speak that which we do know, and testify only to what we have seen.

# Learn of Me!!!

2<sup>nd</sup> Timothy 2:15 say's, "Study to show thyself approved unto God, a workman that need not be ashamed, rightly dividing the word of truth."

This is a profound word to me, because in order to learn how Christ wants us to live, we must take the time to study…just as we do when we want to learn about different professions for our career. In order for you to live for Christ, you must first know what He expects of you. Studying is a special effort to gain knowledge.

In this chapter, Paul gives Timothy advice to help him to remain grounded in Christian service. All Christians need a strong foundation of the Word of God for their ministry. If we are going to train others in the Word of God, we must first know it for ourselves. If we do not study, we cannot make the scriptures a reality to the unbeliever.

If we don't know the Word, we could be subject to leading others who are looking for directions into an area that they were not seeking directions for. It's like someone asking you for directions for getting to Ohio, and you not knowing give them directions that takes them to Virginia. You will be guilty of giving out information that caused them harm.

It is so important to know God's Word, because through his Word we learn how to live our lives for Him, and how to serve Him.

If you know the Word, it will prevent you from being misled by false teachers, and those who have wormed their way in because of the love of money and many other reasons.

Not knowing the Word could cause us to perish because of a lack of knowledge. The scriptures correct us and cause us to walk in the will of God, because through it we get to know God better. Studying has caused me to trust in the Lord with all my heart, and lean not to my own understanding.

Every thing that I go to do, I acknowledge God first. The natural man cannot understand the things of the spirit of God, but the spiritual man has insight to everything. Through studying, we put on the mind of Christ. When was the last time you put in time studying the Word of God? Somehow we just don't take the time that we need to take for studying the Word of God.

When I think about my life, and what an important role the Word of God plays in my life, I can't imagine what I would be like without it because it keeps me whole. Studying God's Word is an important aspect of spiritual growth.

I find that just as we study to acquire knowledge for the different professions of this world, we need to be equally concerned about the knowledge of the Word of God because our lives depend on it. Think about this: it's the Word that saves us.

# *My Testimony*

I will start my testimony by saying, "God is our refuge and strength, a very present help in trouble." (Psalms 46:1) At the beginning of my life, they tell me when I was 2 years old my biological mom passed away and left me motherless, so some would think.

But I was told that after being shifted around for just a little while, this same God placed me into the hands of a loving mother by the name of Mary E. Witherspoon, who was my grandma.

She and my grand–dad Pastor Walter Witherspoon raised me from that point; and made a beautiful, God-fearing intelligent woman of me. Together they gave me a solid faith foundation; and yet the enemy has tried in so many ways to make me feel that this woman was not my mother.

I had to serve notice on the enemy that what God had ordained no man can change. The Word of God does say that if it be of God, no man can over throw it. This thing that God has ordained cannot be altered, changed or voided because there was no paper work. Therefore, it was God's divine will.

I shall forever be grateful to both of them for allowing God to direct them to take me in. This means so much to me even now; when I see the homeless, the foster kids and those who live in the shelters I realize that God found favor in a little once motherless and fatherless child like me.

I encourage everyone that was raised by anyone other than your biological parents to be grateful. This is the will of God concerning you. You should forever be grateful to them; and thankful to God for placing you into the hands of someone who has enough of Gods love in their hearts to take you in.

On June 30, 1996, I was riding down the streets of Milwaukee and there was a young man standing on the street corner, randomly shooting at cars as they passed by. A bullet came through my windshield, went past my head, and landed in the back headrest.

Normally that's where my grandson would have been sitting. By the grace of God he didn't want to go that day, so he stayed behind with Grandpa. After I came to myself, I looked over at my daughter and saw blood in her throat area.

I just knew that she had been shot, but we found that the bleeding was from the shattered glass. When I heard that gun shot, instantly I felt the very presence of God shield me in.

He kept us from all harm. We had no injuries; we didn't even need to go to the hospital; we were kept by God's divine love. I believe His Word even more when I read it now that says "For in the time of trouble, He shall hide me in his pavilion; in the secret of his tabernacle shall He hide me." Every since that day, I trust Him more than ever before. Every time I think about that incident, I just began to praise God for his mighty act of covering us with his blood.

I was so grateful to take an inventory that day and find that our lives were not shattered like the glass from the windshield. For when the enemy came in like a flood to destroy us, the Spirit of God raised a standard against him and protected us from all harm.

# *Watch out God is at work in me!!*

The Word of God says, "Being confident of this very thing, that He which hath begun a good work in me will perform it until the day of Jesus Christ."

"Already you are clean because of the Words that I have spoken to you. Abide in me, and I in you. As the branch cannot bear fruit of itself, unless it abides in the vine, neither can you, unless you abide in me. I am the vine; you are the branches." John 15:3-5.

Look at it this way: If we allow the Word of God to take up residence as to live in us, we can just rest, allowing the Word to work in us and for us. There will be no need to try to work anything out, because the Word says in John 15:5-7, "If you abide in me, and my Word abides in you, ask whatever you wish and it shall be done." I see that we can never try to work independently from Christ.

We must always allow him to work through us and for us. We are all guilty of trying to work things out apart from Christ, or should I say help Christ out. I have learned that there is nothing too hard for God, and if He can't do it; it can't be done.

# *Looking for Help?*

Whenever you need help in any situation, please don't look in the wrong places. Don't look to drugs, alcohol, or any immoralities, but look to the hills from whence cometh your help, and remember that all of your help comes from the Lord who made heaven and earth. (Psalms121:1)

Without God we can do nothing; when we accept that fact, we can rest in him who alone is wisdom. In him we live, we move, and we have our being. For we are his offspring (Acts 17:21)

When your life is just not balancing and you feel weighted with all the cares of this life, let me remind you that we are not the first to struggle with an unbalanced life; therefore, we do not struggle alone. Just remember, others have run the same race and have won it, so don't give up.

We must keep our eyes fixed on the prize of the high calling in Christ Jesus. We have many watching us from the sideline to see how we will handle this race after we've had setbacks during the race. Many times when we are hit by life crisis, we just want to quit right in the middle of the race.

If you quit, there is really no chance of winning, but if you just keep running, you will get to the finish line. Let nothing hold you back. Trust God because he is merciful. Psalms 103:5 says, "He redeems our lives from destruction." He has not dealt with us after our sins, nor rewarded us according to our iniquities. The Bible says in Psalms 103:8 "The Lord is merciful and gracious, slow to anger, and abounding in steadfast love and faithfulness."

This passage paints a beautiful picture of God and His love and compassion towards us, so there is no other person or thing that can match up to the mercy and grace that God shows toward us.

# Preparing to move to the next level

Maybe you have been a Christian for a long time and have become complacent with your level of growth. I am led to believe that there are always higher heights and deeper depths in our Christian walk. For me, growth is moving from one level of faith to another or one place to another.

In our carnal life when we talk about moving, first of all we get very excited! This is how it should be in our Christian life, or do you ever feel the need to move in your Christian life? When we are preparing to move, cleaning is necessary because it is a part of upkeep, and spiritual maintenance.

Often times the Lord has led me to search the closet of my spiritual house. "Brethren, I count not myself to be apprehended: but this one thing I do, forgetting those things which are behind me, and reaching forth unto those things which are before me." (Philippians 3:13)

One day I had to give God ownership of those Sin items that I had packed away in my spiritual closet. They belong to Him. After paying for them with His precious blood, He washed all of my dirty laundry as white as snow. "When the enemy shall come in like a flood, the Spirit of the Lord shall lift up a standard against him." (Isaiah 59:10)

This tells me that the enemy will always be defeated. God's spirit will breathe new life in us as we witness His unending mercy and grace. The Word of God declares that where sin is abounded grace did much more abound.

When we are preparing to move there is so much to get rid off because some of it is worthless, been around too long, and is of no value just taking up space. Just like sin it weighs you down, but if you get rid of it, it's just like obedience; it gives you wings.

The Word of God encourages us to pay attention to our spiritual focus. We must make a point of "fixing our eyes on things that last, the things of God's Kingdom which is the unseen. "For what is seen is temporary, but what is unseen is eternal." Get rid of those boxes of hate, envy, malice, jealousy, un-forgiveness; release fears and increase love and reconciliation.

The more boxes that you have the more room you will need to store them, and you will not have enough space left for the blessings that God has in-store for you. I suggest that we destroy every yoke of bondage that is concealed in those boxes. Make a mad dash for the finish line of forgiveness and set yourself free.

Moving requires keeping our focus. We need to label all boxes correctly because if you are not focusing you could put the wrong label on a box, and when you are ready for the goods that are in that box you won't be able to locate them.

For example, what if you couldn't find love when you need it, what if you couldn't find a box full of peace all because you were not watching where you put it? It's like looking for your keys; you know you put them somewhere but you just don't know where.

Make room for the unending blessings that God is just waiting to give to you such as a clean bill of health, a healthy bank account, and the power of the Holy Ghost. After you have moved to the next level, you are freed and no longer bound by the evil nature.

This means that sin no longer has control over you because you now have the power of God within you and the Word says in 2nd Corinthians 3:17, "Where the spirit of the Lord is there is liberty."

I read in the Word and found out that everybody that the Son set free is free indeed. No longer bound by what others are thinking, saying or even how they treat you. Christ himself came down in a human body just like ours but His body was free from sin and He destroyed sins control; therefore, you can no longer use the statement "the devil made me do it."

Since we moved we now follow after the Holy Spirit that is within us. The Bible says, "If any man be in Christ, he is a new creature: old things are passed away and behold all things are become new." We don't do the things that we used to do, we don't go to the places that we used to go, and we don't live like we used to live, because it's no longer I, but Christ that lives inside of me.

When we have really moved, we begin to follow after the Holy Spirit. We begin to live our lives to please Christ just as Jesus did to please God. When we began to follow after the Holy Spirit, we are really going somewhere.

This leads to a life of peace; it brings us into a spirit of obedience, a spirit of submission, and it leads to life and not death. We begin to have a deeper walk with Christ. Then you can say as Paul said in Romans 8:38-39, "For I am persuaded, that neither death, nor life, nor angels, nor principalities, nor powers, nor things to come; nor height, nor depth, nor any other creature, shall be able to separate me from the love of God, which is in Christ Jesus our Lord.

"I say nothing can separate me from the love of Christ." Now, there was a time that I couldn't say that and be truthful. But today

I can say nothing not worries, pain, misfortune or fame. Maybe you are reading this book and have not moved to the next level in Christ, and maybe moving never crossed your mind.

My advice to you is to let go so you can grow. Let go of all the grudges, quit breathing out bitterness. My girlfriend Lois Green calls it spitting out venom, just down right poison.

Carrying resentment from one year to the next; it's just like dragging around a 370+ pound object; it's tiring you out, it's stealing your joy, it won't let you get any rest at night, and it is damaging you much more than the person that you are angry with.

We need to let go and move forward to the joy that is set before us each day because God is so good to us; until every time we lie down and get up to a new day, we have a new day of grace and mercy.

I had to move because I didn't want to forfeit the blessings that God has in store for me. He puts the smile on my face that no one can erase. If you are not at the proper address when your packages are being delivered, the post man takes it back and he has to try and catch you home in order for you to receive it.

Well, I don't want my package returned for fear of someone else getting it; therefore, I want to be in the proper place when my package of love, hope, joy, or any such thing is delivered, because I can't take the risk of my package being returned or lost. Neither can I risk the chance of it getting delivered to someone else address.

# Don't Just Think Of Yourself

Don't just think about your own affairs, and feelings, but think of others too. You see, the cure for selfishness is servant-hood. A servant is one who is devoted to another, in a subordinate position. Jesus clearly taught that we must deny ourselves if we are going to be His disciples.

In Matthew 16:24 He said, "If anyone would come after me, he must deny himself and take up his cross and follow me." Be careful because man's greatest slavery can be to him-self. In other words, don't do anything out of the flesh.

Reading in the Bible, and from my own experience I found out that self has a big problem. There is a war going on in self that you may not be attentive to; however, the flesh is always at war with the spirit. Sometimes self allows sin to stir up the old sinful nature.

Paul said in Romans 7:18, "For I know that in me (that is in my flesh,) dwelled no good thing" Verse 19 goes on to say, "For the good that I would do, I do not. But the evil which I would not, that I do."

Paul is saying apart from God I can't bring my flesh under submission. It just wants things that I know it doesn't need, but yet I yield to it, it wants me to do things that I know that I shouldn't do, but I sometimes yield, and then again it causes me to say some things that I know are not right to say, but yet I find myself asking for forgiveness for that.

"Beloved, if God so loved us, we ought also to love one another." (I John 4:11) This means we need not pick and choose certain people to love, we must bite the bullet and love even the one's that seems unlovable.

God has truly proven his love for us because God so loved the world that he gave his only begotten Son. This lets me know that our love toward one another must be proven by our actions toward them.

Colossians 3:12-13 says, "Put on therefore, as the elect of God, holy and beloved, bowels of mercies, kindness, humbleness of mind, meekness, longsuffering; Forbearing one another, and forgiving one another, if any man have a quarrel against any even as Christ forgave you, so also do you."

Gods love is unconditional, and the Word of God tells us that his love is in us, and because he has trusted us with His love we cannot be found guilty of hating others. 1 John 4:20-21 says, "If a man says I love God and hate his brother, he is a liar: for he that loves not his brother whom he hath seen, how can he love God that he hath not seen? And this commandment we have from Him, that he who loves God loves his brother also.

# Get A Revelation!

Men ought to always pray, and not faint. Any time without prayer makes one mighty weak. Here Jesus tells the constant need of prayer to show us how important it is to keep praying until your answer comes.

This does not mean endless repetition prayers. It means keeping our request before God until we get an answer, always believing that He will hear and answer our prayers.

# Get A Revelation!

---

"Cast thy bread upon the waters; for thou shall find it after many days." In other words, make sure that you are a good steward over what God has blessed you with, so that you will have what you need in the time of need.

---

# You Were Running Well, Who Cut You Off?

The Lord blessed me to receive a revelation on this topic as I read about Paul's message to the Galatians Christians. These were new Jewish converts who like many of us had made up their minds that they were going to follow Christ as Savior, yet they struggled with their Jewish heritage.

They couldn't make a sound decision of whether to follow the gospel of Jesus Christ or follow the Jewish law. Paul wrote this book calling them back to the gospel of Jesus Christ because they had gotten caught up in the traditions of men and false teachers which led to church controversy.

This is where I see the churches of today and these scriptures came to mind: "O foolish Galatians, who has bewitched you, that you should not obey the truth. Before whose eyes Jesus Christ hath been evidently set forth, crucified among you. Paul was saying your behavior has changed. Who in the world used magic on you or hypnotized you and cast an evil spell upon you?

You need to see the meaning of the death of Jesus Christ as clear as I am waving a picture before your face of the crucifixion. They couldn't see it because of the false teaching and the traditions of men almost as if they had fallen under a spell.

You can agree with me today that this is the way it seems for so many today if the truth be told. Many misuse their stewardship to be crafty, and we just go along to get along as my husband always says.

I am glad that our Word tells us that we should study ourselves; this way we can see what the Word of God is saying to us, and I encourage everyone to study for yourself so when the Word of God is going forth you will be able to follow along and know where to get off if something starts to be interpreted wrongly.

The Bible clearly warns us about the traditions of men because they cause us to nullify what God has said as a direct command and then do the things that are pleasing to us. The international Bible calls them man made rules.

In the 15th chapter of Matthew the Scribes and the Pharisees went to Jesus saying, "Why do the disciples transgress against the tradition of the elders? For they wash not their hands when they eat bread."

Jesus answered and said unto them, "why do ye also transgress the commandment of God by your traditions? For God commanded, saying, honor thy father and mother and, he that curses father or mother, let him die the death."

"But ye say, whosoever shall say to his father or his mother, it is a gift, by whatsoever thou might be profited by me; and honor not his mother, he shall be free. Thus have ye made the commandment of God of none effect by your tradition."

The Pharisees questioned Jesus' authority because they knew the religious tradition of men and that's the way many of us are today; we won't study because we want to stay in good grace with others so therefore we figure it's better that we don't know the truth because I found out that the truth separates us from those who want to live in darkness rather than in the light.

The Pharisees had added hundreds of religious traditions to God's law and wanted the people of God to abide by them. Mind you, many traditions are not bad but they never supersede the Word of God.

Because if God said it, you better believe it, and let that settle it. Tradition can some time give good morals but they can never save you. The other scripture that comes to mind is Galatians 5:7 "Ye did run well; who did hinder you that ye should not obey the truth?" I saw myself this way, running well and then I got cut off because I heard too many traditions.

If you don't read and receive the Truth from God instead of listen to men's traditions, you can really get cut off as in hindered because you yourself don't really know what the Word of God is saying to you. And when you don't know what God's Word is saying and what God expects of you, you can become bound by the tradition of men.

The Word of God does say. You shall know the Truth and the Truth shall make you free. This means when you know that you know, what you know you know, that's when you know that you do know.

No matter who says it, if its mom or dad, friends or love ones. If it's not what the Word says then you need to be found believing and doing what the Word says you should do. This is in any situation, because the Word of God always takes precedence over any and everyone's opinions.

We ignore Gods specific order in order to follow our own traditions. Some are so entrenched in their traditions that they cannot accept the move of Christ. Some other things that cuts us off are marital problems, financial problems, health problems, church problems, children problems, envy, hate, misunderstanding, jealousy, adultery, fornication, etc.

The enemy will use whatever he can to distract you from getting what God has for you. You yourself know that when things are not going well in your life, this takes your focus off your spiritual walk with the Lord and starts the mind game of "what if."

When we don't have money, you know that it seems like every thing stops. You stop living almost; some can't take it and commit suicide. They figure life is no longer worth living. We forget all about what the Word says in Philippians 4:19: "But my God shall supply all your needs according to his riches in glory by Christ Jesus."

No matter what our situations may be, we can always trust that God will meet every one of our needs because we know that God said it in his word and no matter what, His Word doesn't lie. I read where it says that before God lie both heaven and earth will pass away.

*Step into MY Poetry*

# All That I have Left Is Memories

The laughter, the love and the great morals are now clouding my memory. They are all I have left since you had to go away and leave me. I still have the memories of how you took me in when others were too busy for me.

You were very patient, kind, loving and understanding. Because of your training, I know that in life I will succeed. All I have now are those wonderful memories of what was, since you had to go away. Don't get me wrong I know that it was no choice of yours.

I will dry my eyes now and mourn no more. You left me such memories to enjoy. Remembering those days that we shared and enjoyed peacefully-I can appreciate, celebrate and not grieve. You taught me how to love others and myself. You gave me high self-esteem. Now, because of that, great memories are left to me.

In loving memory of Mary E. Witherspoon

Copyright © 2007 Evangelist Jessie B. Clay

# *Until I've Been Discovered*

An inspirational writer, this is what I was really born to be. Right now, no one knows it but me. But I must make it known somehow.

There is so much encouragement stored inside me, and I would love to give it to others. If you know about inspirational encouragement then we can encourage each other.

Today I am making an effort to make my writing abilities known. Now you won't have to go looking for it, because technology has placed it into your home.

I'll just keep writing inspirationally, until someone discovers a great and inspiring writer like me.

Don't be too critical to make this great discovery! Because when I am rich and famous, you will have missed the opportunity to say that you were the one that published me.

## *I know you've Been Waiting*

I know that you've been waiting for your dreams to come true. By now, you are wondering why it's taking so long, because you feel in your heart that it's long overdue.

A dream is something that we must follow after or pursue; doing everything within our power to make it a reality-come true. Now don't go thinking that I am just a writer, with no concerns about you.
Just know that I am writing because like you, I've been waiting for my dreams to come true. Now I am making an effort to follow, and pursue.

# I Will Prevail!

I have decided to take life in stride. I'm going to stay humble and always swallow my pride. On my honor, I will strive to make the best of whatever life brings my way, no longer fighting for the wrong choices I've made so many times along the way.

I have decided to take life as it comes and goes. Because through my experiences I have learned that I can't bring anyone other than myself to order or under control.

Now I will give birth to the writing skills that have been entrusted to me. This type of writing I've learned is what many in the world today long for, and really need to read. Be encouraged.

# God Meant It for My Good

Once I was so restless in my spirit that I couldn't find peace anywhere. I had a racing spirit within me, and I was always on the go because Satan was using things that I didn't want to deal with, or face reality about to keep me on the move. Sometimes in life, there are things that happen to us that we really don't want to face the truth about.

The pressures of life were weighing me down so heavily until one day when I went to the dentist; he said to me, "You have been gritting your teeth at night while you were asleep." Then he asked a question: "Is there something bothering you?" I answered that question to myself because I knew that I was troubled on every side.

The dentist told me, "Whatever it is, you really need to let it go. "I went home and went into my prayer room and gave it all to God in prayer and I totally surrendered my life to the Lord. I want to let you know that when you totally surrender your life to the Lord you will find out that the devil meant it for bad, but God turned it around for your good.

I had to go through, in order to get to, where God wanted me to be. Because if I never had a problem, I wouldn't know that He can solve them and that my trials only come to make me strong.

And now I can say this: For the time of God's favor has come. All that mourn will receive joy instead of mourning; will be given beauty for their ashes, and praise instead of heaviness. The down trodden shall be freed from their oppressor, and God is ready to give blessings to all who come to him; Instead of shame and dishonor, you will enjoy a double share of honor Isaiah (61:3-7).

God has equipped me to encourage all who need encouraging; just in case you have gone through storms like me, I need to remind you that although storms don't stop coming, "I have never seen a storm that didn't pass over."

I must testify, though, because of the storms that I have encountered, I have learned that they are designed to push us toward the destiny that God has ordained for us. Make sure your life is built on the solid foundation of Jesus Christ, a strong, solid foundation that stands firm when storms come.

I appreciate everything that happen to me that caused me to line up with the Word of God, and I can truly say what my mom said and that is "a lesson taught is better than a lesson bought." Once you have gone through, you can pass that wisdom on to others and if they accept it, they will come out much better than you did.

No matter how far down that you think you are or how far off track you think you are, God is still right there for you. All you need to do if you have not accepted Him as your Savior is do it today.

He is not like your relatives or friends, who are not willing to forgive you or let it die, or always reminding you of your past... like they don't have one. I think that the reason why they want to keep you focusing on your past is so you can forget about theirs.

I have learned one thing and that is "The only people that don't have skeletons in their closets are the ones that still have live sin in their lives." In other words, they are still doing what they were doing and that is living in sin.

# Release the Hurts of Your Past

Through my ministry I have learned that there are so many people hurting because they just can't find it in their hearts to forgive their offender. Many marriages have been destroyed and those individuals actually end up in a much worse situation all because they couldn't release the hurt from their past.

Once we have closed one season we must get ready for the new season. This means we can't carry anything from the season that's already past into the next season. Isaiah 43:18-19 says, "Remember ye not the former things, neither consider the things of old."

Behold, I will do a new thing; now it shall spring forth; shall ye not know it? I will even make a way in the wilderness, and rivers in the deserts, to give drink to my people, my chosen." Isaiah encourages us to leave behind the old life. This means we need to forget everything that the enemy has done to us.

I mean completely throw it out of our minds, all those things about how mom gave you away, how family members mistreated you, how the in-laws don't care for you; whatever you feel that your misfortunes are or have been.

If you keep holding on to the hurt and pain regarding the bad things that have happened to you in life, when something good does happen you won't realize it because you are so busy allowing your dark past to cover up your bright future that God has in store for you.

You may be saying. "How can I forget the former things?" 2nd Corinthians 10:5 says, "Casting down imaginations, and every high thing that exalts itself against the knowledge of God, and bringing into captivity every thought to the obedience of Christ."

Stop remembering the bad things that someone has done to you because it only hurts you. It causes depression, hypertension, discouragement and many other health problems. We see in this scripture that we have the power to take our thoughts captive.

We need to break out into a season of reconciling relationships. Un-forgiveness is one of the most damaging things to our health because not only does it hurt us physically but spiritually as well. The Bible warns us against it and tells us how important it is to forgive.

Matthew 6:14-15 lets us know just how important it is for us to forgive each other; in fact, our salvation depends on it. It says, "For if ye forgive men their trespasses, the heavenly Father will also forgive you: But if ye forgive not men their trespasses, neither will your Father forgive your trespasses."

If you don't forgive and release the hurt from your past, you cause a great struggle within yourself because no doubt the person you are holding the grudge against has forgiven you and moved on because even though you may not want to have anything to do with them after they have made every effort to reconcile with you and you have refused because you think that they are not worthy to be forgiven, God still forgives them.

I need to tell you if you have tried to reconcile with someone and they are not accepting and releasing you, don't be weary in your well doing. To be "weary" means to be worn out in strength and endurance…to be tired. You could be weary both physically and mentally.

You have tried everything, you have gone to them so many times until you feel that your strength seems to be giving out, and you are about ready to give up and throw in the towel. When you start to feel this way you need to be reminded of the above scripture.

Once I spent many restless nights because I had asked someone for forgiveness who didn't think that I should be forgiven. I tried everything. I made phone calls; I sent letters and cards however, nothing was good enough it made things worse. By the grace of God I was able to get free of that situation and moved on.

I needed to write about this because not only are there some who don't want to forgive, but there are some who are waiting to be forgiven and the other party is not willing to forgive because the enemy is using this situation as a tool to keep them miserable and in bondage and they may not be aware of it. Things like this sometimes separate spouses, family member, and friends.

Sometime we reach out for people who just don't want us to be a part of their lives and this brings stress to our lives, but I am reminding you that you must not let Satan use this as a tool against you any longer. Go ahead and break bondage; set yourself free.

The fact that others don't want you to be a part of their circle does not mean that something is wrong with you; sometimes it means that you are walking in a different direction and you can only hang with your kind.

This doesn't mean that they hate you. I always say, "They don't hate me; they just love me so much until they don't know how to express their love for me." Let me warn you that life is really too short to have all of these unnecessary issues going on.

I had the opportunity to minister to a friend of mine who told me she has a brother who for no reason that they knew off stopped coming around, or talking to any of his sisters for 20 years. When they finally got the chance to ask him why, they found out that he was struggling within himself about something from the past.

I am happy to say that this brother now lives with one of his sisters and the struggle is over. My question to you is how long and at what point do you stop and deal with your unfinished past struggles that lies within you?

Some of his sisters had passed on and didn't get the opportunity to witness the confession that he made, so don't let it be said too late. If you confess your faults God is just to forgive you. It doesn't matter how long it took you to do it; all that matters is that you do it before it's too late.

I really want to caution everyone against passing grudges on to your children and others. You know how it is when we are angry with someone; we want everyone to stop associating with them just because we don't want to have anything to do with them. It becomes a generational curse. Go ahead break the curse before it get started.

# *Everybody Has Trouble*

Through the Word of God, Jesus tells us that in the world we will have tribulations, but He encourages us to be of good cheer because He overcame the world. According to the dictionary, the word *tribulation* means great misery or distress as from oppression; deep sorrow, suffering, afflictions; and trials.

The word *overcome* is defined as getting the better of in a struggle or conflilct; and conquer; and defeat: to *over power the enemy.* When we begin to have problems, even as adults, we feel very intimidated, embarrassed, discouraged and weak, because the enemy tells us that no one else is experiencing this type of problem or any problem for that matter.

It seems as though everyone around us is living a perfect life: for example, to us all couples appear to be perfect couples, but you and your spouse seem to be having all kinds of troubles. It seems as if their children are smarter, more intelligent, listens to their parents, and are well-behaved; well, this is the way the enemy deceives us.

It seems to you as if your child is not making much progress in the direction that you think he or she should be going, and it seems as if your child has no plans or goals toward the greater things in life.

Then there are those neighbors, friends, and family members who put their mouths on you and your child hurting you even more.

Maybe you are going through this right now. In other words it seems as if you are the only one having problems.

Let me assure you that although these people may not be experiencing the same type of problems that you are experiencing at this time, nevertheless; you can be certain that they do have a problem of some kind.

If we were smart we would keep our mouths shut when others are having problems because if we speak wrongly about others while they are suffering we will reap whatever we sow.

Your children may be the ones acting crazy now, but if others have children, there is a great chance that if they haven't already showed out on them; they should just keep quiet and brace themselves.

Although you may not be experiencing any difficulties at the same time others are, if you are still here you know what has happened to you in the past, but you have no way of knowing what lies ahead for you in the future.

James 1:2 says, "My brethren, count it all joy when ye fall into divers temptation." Here the word "temptation" is referring to trials and tests only, not enticement to do the wrong thing.

This scripture implies that we will have difficult times, but we need to be reminded that we can profit from them. My testimony is that I am stronger than I have ever been, and that is because I have had so many trials in my life, and the more trials I have the stronger I get. I am sure now that I can weigh the size of my blessing by the size of the trial that I am experiencing.

If I am experiencing a big trial then I know in my spirit that I am going to receive a big blessing. The third verse of James 1 says, "Knowing this, that the trying of your faith worketh patience."

I have found out that it means just what it says when it says "worketh patience." It's like being placed on the potter's wheel being made over again.

It's easy to find joy when everything is going well, but what about when we have been sacked by the enemy? When we are having a bad morning that's easy to endure, but what about when we are hit two to three consecutive days and then days turn into weeks etc.?

It could be that you are tired of fighting, and just fed up because it seems that nothing you do ever turn out right. Maybe you are giving up and want to throw in the towel because you seem to be fighting unending battles.

I encourage you not to lose your joy because if you don't have joy, you have no strength to fight back. The Bible says in Nehemiah 8:10 that the joy of the Lord is our strength. In other words, we are strengthened in our spirit when we have joy.

With the joy that I have, Satan can no longer get the same reaction from me today that he has gotten from me in the past after facing certain trials, because I have been strengthened in those areas.

Since I have the joy that produces strength; I can now love my enemies, bless them that curse me, do good to those that hate me, and pray for those who despitefully use me and persecute me.

No matter how saved we are or what our status is in this world, how rich we are, or even how poor, we will face some adversities, crisis, and hardships. I want to warn you that you must not fall from the faith when you are faced with such.

I want you to be encouraged and not faint when bad things happen to you. Please be aware that it's not like we have heard that we only suffer because we have done something wrong. That's not always the case. Just know that you will have trials no matter what. Jesus suffered, and He had done no wrong.

Sometimes my faith gets shaken as well, but I have the knowledge of Christ which pulls me up out of every horrible pit. The Bible lets us know that we do perish due to a lack of knowledge. If I didn't have the knowledge of Christ I know that I would surely break under pressure.

The knowledge of Christ helps me to understand why I must go through tribulations and trials. It also lets me know how to save myself from Satins attacks. James 4:7 says, "Submit yourselves to God. Resist the devil, and he will flee from you." This mean don't give Satan the time of day because all he wants to do is kill, steal, and destroy us.

Since I have spoken to you about the trials, I need to speak to you about the peace that is talked about within the same verse. God will keep you in perfect peace if you keep your mind off your trials, and on Him.

You can have peace now knowing that trials produce Godly character: patience, perseverance hope, and praise. When you are faced with a trial in the future you won't need to try and explain the reason for the trial, because you know now that it just might be for divine purpose.

"All things work together for the good of them who love God, to them who are the called according to his purpose" (Romans 8:28). Keep in mind that God is going to turn it around to work in your favor.

If you let patience have her perfect work, the Word says you won't have to want for anything. "Blessed is the man that endures temptation: for when he is tried, he shall receive the crown of life, which the Lord has promised to them that love Him.”

My aim is to help everyone understand that no one can guarantee you that you won't have trouble because Jesus did and He said you will. There is absolutely no way of avoiding having bad things happen to us no matter how good we are.

When trouble does come our way we don't have to let our hearts be troubled, neither let it be afraid. We can just rest in the arms of Jesus and have peace because He left his peace with us, not as the world gives but as Christ gives.

In the book of John 14:27, we can read where Jesus said “Peace I leave with you, my peace I give unto you: not as the world give, give I unto you.” This comfort was left to us by Jesus so don't allow your heart to be troubled or afraid. We must tap into this divine peace.

You can find this peace that I am referring to in Christ alone. Every time I get weary in my well-doing I think about this peace, and when I think of this peace, my heart starts to leap for Joy, and I am no longer fearful about whatever is going on around me.

We have no way of knowing what we will be faced with tomorrow. However, we have no need to fear the present or the future because this peace is an assurance in any circumstance; we have the blessed assurance that although it may be too hard for us it's not too hard for God, the problem solver.

If your life is filled with stress, fear, doubt, or any other things that may be causing you discomfort just allow God to fill your mind with His true peace. I know that it seems as if it's impossible for you to think of not having to worry about anything. The Bible tells us not to worry because worrying will not change anything, and it reveals a lack of faith.

What's the point of worrying? Luke 12: 25-26 says, "And which of you with taking thought can add to his stature one cubit? "If ye then be not able to do that thing which is least, why take ye thought for the rest?"

We need to focus on not putting any more time into worrying, but turn it around and began to put all the time that we have been spending on worrying into praying and reading the Word of God. Whenever you start to worry, just stop and begin to pray.

Once I was troubled about a situation that had occurred with one of my adult children and to me this one was really big and I knew that because of negligence something drastic could happen.

You know how we are about our children no matter how old they are we still worry about them. We are very concerned, protective, and we love them so much until we don't want any thing bad to happen to them. We want the best for them.

I begin to read the Word and pray. Then one night while I was sleeping, I heard the Spirit say "Psalm 24:7." I didn't want to interrupt my sleep by getting up to read what this scripture was saying.

I locked this scripture in my mind and fell back to sleep and the Spirit spoke again saying "Psalm 9." I locked this scripture in my memory bank as well because I wanted to know what God was telling me through His Word about my situation.

I rose up early the next morning and opened the Bible to read what God was saying to me through His Word, and this is what it said in Psalm 24:7: "Lift up your head, oh ye gates; and be ye lifted up, ye everlasting doors, and the king of glory shall come in." To me this meant the Lord had heard my prayer and seen my tears, and given me the victory over that situation.

The Spirit dealt with me and shared with me that as parents with adult children we spend way too much time worrying about things that we can't do anything about, and in the first place, we need to recognize that they are no longer kids. These are adults who are responsible for their own actions, and must be held accountable.

We can only instruct them with the best advice; we cannot force them to make the choices that we think they should make. The Spirit also said that because of the distractions by our children, the wife can't be the wife that she needs to be to her husband, nor can the husband be the husband that he needs to be to his wife because the enemy is using this to bring division in marriages.

My prayer now is Lord sustain me while you work on my children and all of my situations. Sometimes the situation doesn't change, but if your attitude toward that situation changes this will give you great relief.

I am sure that we have disappointed our parents at some point in our lives, but in most cases we were chastened by God and through that process we became children of obedience. We as parents go though so much trying to keep God from chastening our adult children. We can relax knowing it will only make them better like it did us.

1st Peter 5:10 says, "After we have suffered for a while, our God, who is full of kindness through Christ, will give us his eternal glory. He will come and pick us up, and personally set us firmly in place, and make us stronger than ever."

I trust God to do everything that I need Him to do for me, and that's why I asked Him to sustain me so I don't get into areas where I don't belong. I begin to see my situations in the future and they really do look so much better.

Every day I feel God supernaturally sustaining me. Sometimes I feel like He is my super natural handyman. I see Him working in my house, fixing on things that He sees needing to be fixed, building things that need to be built, and putting things back together that were almost utterly destroyed.

When I talk to others I discover He's working in their homes as well. He specializes in giving us grace when we need it. Psalm 55:22 says, "Cast thy burden upon the Lord, and He shall sustain thee; He shall never suffer the righteous to be moved."

In this scripture the Lord invites us to give our burdens to Him; He wants to carry them for us. Thank God that the same strength that carries us can carry our burdens.

Weeping may endure for a night, but I am so glad that joy comes in the morning. It's like a shot given by your doctor, the discomfort is momentary, but the affects of the shot makes you feel better, and that part of it last for a long time.

# Never Give Up On God

God always come through on time. I don't care how long you think that it's taking Him; my answer is still the same. Sometimes our problems seem so large for us but when it's too large for us, it's just right for God. God is able to do exceedingly abundantly above all that we can ask or think, according to the power that works in us.

Maybe you have been diagnosed with a terminal illness, maybe you've lost a job, you may be on the verge of foreclosure, it may look like your marriage is about to end and God knows it may seem that your child is just not getting it. I encourage you to hold on and rest in the promises of God.

Every time the enemy brings the thought of your problems to your mind just say Lord I believe your Word because His Word doesn't lie. Numbers 23:19 says "God is not a man, that He should lie; neither the son of man that He should repent: hath He said, and shall He not do it? Or hath He spoken, and shall He not make it good?"

God does not change His mind like humans do and He has never made a promise without fulfilling it. There are many stories in the Bible that I can refer to in order to prove my point not to mention when I look at my life and how He never failed me.

Not one time when my bills were due, not one time when the doctor gave me a bad report, not one time when the enemy tried to take my job. I can agree with the Word that says the Lord will provide. 2$^{nd}$ Peter 3:9 says " The Lord is not slack concerning His promise, as some men count slackness; but is longsuffering to us ward."

Trust me God is really the kind of person that I want to hang around me because I found out that He will do everything that He said that He would do. If you need a Bible witness I will share this story with you and you can open the Bible and read it for yourself.

God promised Abraham and Sarah a son and He repeated His promise several times. Abraham thought that they had gotten too old; he and his wife even tried to help God out and really made a mess for themselves just as we sometimes do.

When Abraham was 99 years old and Sarah was nearly that old the Lord paid them a visit and told them that the time had come for their son to come. Sarah laughed because she thought that she was too old. But sure enough God sent them a little boy, and they named him Isaac. Abraham and Sarah were so happy they had a feast in order to show him to all of their friends.

After reading this story I learned that if God say He is going to do something for us, we need to learn how to wait on God. While we are waiting our strength is being renewed according to the Word of God and we can mount up with wings as eagles.

After God has proved Himself to us we can run and not be weary; walk and not faint. We all need to learn how to wait because like Abraham and Sarah when we try to help God out we make the biggest mess ever. He has proved himself time and time again that's why I have come to the place where I can just stand on His Word and wait.

Read I Samuel chapter one, about Hannah a woman of prayer who prayed and waited patiently on the Lord to come to her rescue and He did. Hannah was barren, childless, and in deep distress, she made a vow that if God would only give her a son, she would give him back to the Lord all the days of his life.

Hannah had every reason to be stressed out because her husbands other wife Peninnah had children and she would always laugh at Hannah at the festivals making her cry. At that time you were thought to be a failure if you couldn't have children.

Hannah spent time in the temple after that crying out to the Lord, asking Him to look on her afflictions and remember her. Hannah prayed until something happen. The Lord remembered her petition and blessed her with a boy child named Samuel.

Not only did God bless her with a boy child but with six other children. This tells me that if you call on the Lord, meaning it from your heart, and wait, He will come.

If you are deeply troubled like Hannah was, why not use the same method that she used to get her burdens lifted, her tears wiped away, and her prayer answered. In times past I know that I gave up too easily when my prayers were not answered when I thought that they should be.

At that time I was not as sure as I am now about the power that I possess through Jesus Christ our Lord. Now that I have studied and know Gods Word, I have mounted up with wings as an eagle.

The enemy can no longer bully me around since I found out that I am the head and not the tail, above and not beneath, I have the power to resist and above all I am the King's kid.

After God had blessed Hannah with the child that she asked for, the Bible said she began to thank and praise God through a song. In other words she showed Him gratitude for answering her prayer.

This is what we should do when God blesses us with things that we have asked him for and He grants them to us. We must not forget what God has done for us but we must make known his deeds among the people.

I would like to bring this a step closer to you by telling you about a taunting situation that occurred with me while working in the cooperate world. There was an incident where the enemy used a supervisor to taunt me about my job.

As far as I could tell the struggle was within her because I was never late for work and I could never afford to miss a day because I needed the money so badly. But sometimes when you are so happy it just irks others; especially when they know that you are struggling and they think you should be unhappy because of it.

Anyway, she decided that I should be fired. She called me into her office along with other staff members being present and presented her case as to why I should be fired. Instantly I began to pray in my spirit because heaven knew that I really needed my job.

I must tell you that I didn't have to say anything in my defense because God sent a representative on my behalf who said I see no reason to fire this woman. The supervisor said well, she's not reaching productivity then my representative said due to her excellent work record it seems to me your only option would be to find her another position.

That supervisor still harboring a grudge against me then demoted me. I made a vow that I would get fresher under pressure. Some of my co-workers suggested that I quit, but God gave me the strength to overcome that set back. I was promoted to a higher position in another department, at a higher pay rate and stayed there nine years. That supervisor was demoted after I left her department. We really need to be careful what we do to others because it could come back to hunt us. The Bible does say that we will reap what we sow.

Through this experience I learned that what the enemy meant to be a set back against me, God meant it to be a setup for another blessing. Just when you think that you can't make it through and you feel like all of your hope is gone, remember that God knows, He sees, and He cares for you.

# *Tell A Friend*

Now that you have made it to this page, I am asking that you would spread the word to others about this book, telling them how you felt when you started at the beginning, and how you feel now that you have completed reading it.

I pray that something that you have read in this book has given you a new outlook on your spiritual walk with the Lord causing you to be stronger than you have ever been before.

"God is our refuge and strength, a very present help in trouble. Therefore, we will not fear, though the earth is removed, and though the mountains are carried into the midst of the sea." (Psalm 46:1-2) You can count on God.